The Armour of God

James Poole

ISBN: 978-1-78364-319-6

THE OPEN BIBLE TRUST
Fordland Mount, Upper Basildon,
Reading, RG8 8LU, UK.

www.obt.org.uk

The Armour of God

Contents

The Armour of God   4

Introduction

INTRODUCTION

God's plan and purpose is the Reconciliation of all, in the Heavens and in the Earth, through the blood of Christ's cross (Colossians 1:20). It is in the heavenly realms that Christ's Body has a part to play and those of us who have grasped by faith our calling which is above in Christ Jesus, find that we are up

> "against the principalities, powers, rulers of the darkness of this age, against spiritual hosts of wickedness in the heavenly places" (Ephesians 6:12).

They very much resent our intrusion into their realm. Hence there is the need for Divine Armour to protect us in our conflict with them, as they seek to prevent us from enjoying, by faith, God's inheritance in the saints. (His allotment among the saints CV (the Concordant Version) - Ephesians 1:18.) Unlike Israel we do not possess an earthly territory, but we do possess, *in Christ,* territory in the heavenly realms:

"For our citizenship (realm CV) is in the heavens, from whence (KJV) we also eagerly wait for the Saviour, the Lord Jesus Christ, Who will transform our lowly body (body of humiliation CV), that it may be conformed to His glorious body, according to the working by which He is able to subdue all things to Himself". (Philippians 3:20-21 RAV)

We cannot be robbed of our allotment in the heavens, for it is *in Christ* and we are *in Him*, but our Adversary, Satan, can rob us of the *enjoyment of it* if we do not stand, *by faith,* on the territory God has given us in Christ.

Our standing in Christ is the same for all of God's saints, the weakest as well as the most mature. It is a matter of *grace,* not knowledge. The babe in Christ has just as strong a titlehold to the heavenly allotment, as the most illustrious and mature saint. But, alas, there are many of the Lord's dear people, who "mind earthly things". They prefer milling round in territory that does not belong to them. They appropriate to themselves the privileges and responsibilities of Israel, God's chosen earthly people, being ignorant of their true calling which is *in Christ Jesus in the heavenly realms*. Paul shed many tears for them and so should we! We are told to stand and withstand all who seek to dislodge us from the enjoyment of our heavenly allotment in Christ.

In the KJV, we have the words "withstand" and "stand" (Ephesians 6:13-14). The Holy Spirit is emphasising something very important. Our warfare is a *defensive* one. There is no command to advance to the attack. We are told to hold on to *by faith,* what we have been given by *grace in Christ*.

When Israel occupied the Promised Land, they frequently had to defend it against the nation they had displaced.

When faith in The Lord and obedience to His will prevailed, they were victorious over their adversaries.

When they departed from following The Lord, they were defeated. On such occasions, He raised up men of faith and valour who by faith and obedience, led the nation of Israel once more to overcome their enemies. The book of Judges is full of such names - Gideon, Deborah, and Barak, Samson.

Are there not needed today men of faith, to point to the heavenly allotment many of the saints have forsaken and enlighten them of their true calling in Christ Jesus? Praise the Lord there are a few who, like Joshua and Caleb, wholly follow The Lord.

Now how can we hold on to our heavenly allotment by faith? We need to be "strong in the Lord and the power of His might". The *power* of His might consists in an armour or panoply and if we put it on it provides us with complete protection from all our foes. We *are* living in an evil day where there is so much departure from the faith once given to the saints.

The Armour of God   10

1.
The Belt of
Truth

1. THE BELT OF TRUTH

The belt covers a vital part of the body, the loins (waist) which the dictionary defines as that part of the body on both sides of the spine, between the ribs and the hipbones. A wound caused here by a shaft of the adversary Satan is fatal. Without truth we are in darkness and error. Our Lord said, "I and the Truth" (John 14:6). The written Word of God, which points to the Living word, Christ, must be "rightly divided" (2 Timothy 2:15).

All of God's Word is truth, but not all of His truth can be directly applied to us, members of Christ's Body. We do not know "Christ according to the flesh", (2 Corinthians 5:16), that is His particular relationship to Israel, God's chosen earthly people. Much truth proclaimed by our Lord on earth belongs to Israel exclusively, although it is for our instruction, (2 Timothy 3:16-17).

On the other hand, there is much *basic* truth in the Old Testament, Gospels, Acts, the Epistle to the Hebrews, and the letters of James, Peter, John, Jude and the book of Revelation, which can be applied in *all* God's dispensations.

Even Paul's epistles need to be "rightly divided", between those written before Acts 28:26-28 and those written from prison in Rome. The former contain the foundation stones for the "prison epistles", e.g., justification by faith, reconciliation to God and a new creation of believing Jews and Gentiles into one Body.

The dispensational characteristics belonging to them, such as healing, tongues and other

Pentecostal powers have passed away. Maturity has arrived with Paul's later epistles written from his Roman prison: Ephesians, Philippians, Colossians, 2 Timothy, (1 Timothy seems to overlap the earlier and later epistles). A prayerful study of all Paul's epistles, will enable us to "approve (test) the things that are excellent" ("test what things are of consequence" CV) Philippians 1:10.

In other words, some things are to be discarded, and others, which are in accord with maturity in Christ Jesus, kept. We are "complete in Him" (Colossians 2:9-23). All the rites and ceremonies of former dispensations are a shadow of the reality which we, as members of Christ's Body, have in Him.

2.

The Breastplate

of

Righteousness

2. THE BREASTPLATE OF RIGHTEOUSNESS

The breastplate or cuirass of righteousness is the next piece of armour to put on. It covered the Roman soldier from front to back, encasing all his vital organs in a coat of mail. God's Righteousness is our breastplate in which we are protected all round against the assaults of the Adversary, Satan. It is "apart from law", a Righteousness of God, by faith of Jesus Christ (*Christ's* faith), unto all and upon all them that believe, for there is no difference (distinction), for *all* have sinned and come short of the glory of God" (Romans 3:21-23 KJV).

In the book of Judges, there is a description of 700 soldiers of the tribe of Benjamin who, it is said, could sling a stone at a hair's breadth and never miss the target (Judges 20:16). It is a remarkable thing that the Hebrew word *Chata*, translated "miss" in this context is translated "sin" in other parts of the Old Testament.

So here we have a true definition of sin. It is to iss the mark, to come short of perfection. We have a saying, "a miss is as good as a mile". The fact that we may be better than others, that is - not miss the mark by so much - is irrelevant before God. We have come short. We have sinned and the recognition of this is the start of the Christian life. We are found:

> "in Him (Christ), not having our own righteousness, which is of the law but that which is through faith in (of) Christ (His *faith*), the righteousness which is from God by (*for our*) *faith*" (Philippians 3:9).

We have a righteous standing before God, *in Christ,* which does not vary, but, in order to defeat our spiritual foes, we must live righteously, in the power of Christ's resurrection life or else we shall suffer some wounding by our adversary, Satan. Unrighteous acts condemn us in the sight of both men and our spiritual adversaries. We shall also incur loss at the dais of Christ, when our walk and service are assessed by Him (1 Corinthians 3:13-15).

"For we are His workmanship (achievement CV), created in Christ Jesus for good works, which God prepared beforehand that we should walk in them". (Ephesians 2:10)

3.

The Sandals of Peace

3. THE SANDALS OF PEACE

In Romans 11:15, we are told "their (Israel) being cast away is the reconciliation of the world". Actually this is a *one-sided conciliation.* (Greek *Katallage*), on God's part. When His conciliatory attitude is received by individuals who lay aside their enmity, then there *is reconciliation: two sided* (Greek *Apokatallage*). *The Concordant Version* clearly shows this distinction, which is not shown in other versions e.g., *Conciliation* Romans 5:11, Romans 11:15, 2 Corinthians 5:18-

19; *reconciliation.* Ephesians 2:16, Colossians 1:20 and 21.

We who have received the conciliation are at peace with God and in the light of His present attitude to mankind, we should imitate Him by putting on the sandals of peace towards mankind. God does not take into account their trespasses (offences CV) against Him, so we should not take into account mankind's offences against us (2 Corinthians 5:19).

It is not always easy to adopt such a peaceful attitude towards some of our fellow believers and unbelievers. The flesh in us gets irritated and vexed so that, alas, at times we do not have on the sandals of peace. The more we are conscious of our unworthiness and God's super-abounding grace to ourselves, then the more we are encouraged to be like our Heavenly Father: to walk in love, not taking offence at the words and actions of our fellow men. Paul gives us a guide in 2 Timothy 2:24-26.

"... and a servant of The Lord must not quarrel but be gentle to all, apt to teach, patient, in humility correcting those who are in opposition, if perhaps God will grant them repentance, so that they may know the truth, and that they may come to their senses and escape the snare of the Devil, having been taken captive by him to do his will". (RAV)

What a wonderful attitude of peace is shown by Paul. He was accused of crimes which he did not commit: a Roman citizen, cast into prison and bound by a chain to a Roman soldier. Did he complain about his treatment? No, he glorified in the fact that he was not just a prisoner of Rome, *but of The Lord!* He rejoiced that his bonds in Christ had helped the furtherance of the gospel and emboldened the brethren at Philippi to speak the Word of God fearlessly (Philippians 1:12-14). And from his prison were written the most sublimes and most transcendent revelations of Christ's exalted Headship and *our exaltation in Him!* (Ephesians 1:19-23). Here was a man whose heart and mind were at peace with God and mankind!

4.

The Shield of Faith

4. THE SHIELD OF FAITH

This is not the small shield used in hand to hand combat. One could compare it to the large shields used by our own riot police, against violent mobs that throw things at them. Such a large shield is ours, to protect us from the missiles of our adversary, Satan. Note that this is the large shield of *the* Faith, (the definite article is there in the Greek). Although all God's Word, "rightly divided", is a shield for us, yet it is the *particular* faith that Paul has brought us in his prison epistles, embodied in Christ Jesus our Lord, our risen, ascended, and seated Lord of Glory, our great Shield of Faith!

In ancient warfare elephants were used to rout the enemy by their onslaught. To combat this a counter device was invented. Arrows were fitted with combustibles, lit and shot into the thick hide of the animals, who became so terror stricken by the blazing darts and maddened by their burning wounds, that they stampeded, doing more damage to their own side than to the enemy.

Our spirit foes use such fiery darts to wound and torture us. Only faith in our great Shield, Christ Jesus, can ward off the darts before they harm us. He is our "Shield and Hiding place", from all Satan's attempts to wound us! Speaking personally, I have found Christ Jesus complete protection from misquoted Scripture and all manner of accusations. But one must not get complacent. How true it is that "pride goes before destruction and a haughty spirit before a fall" (Proverbs 16:18).

The Armour of God   26

5.

The Helmet of Salvation

5. THE HELMET OF SALVATION

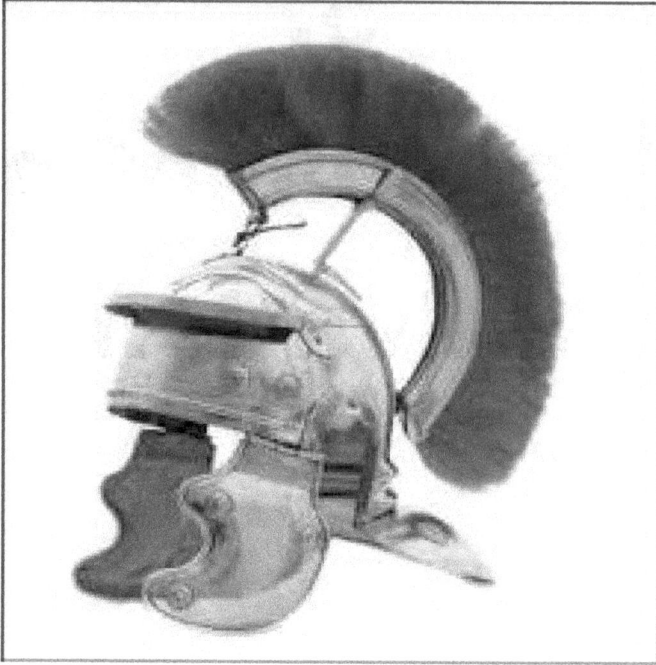

Salvation has more than one aspect. There is salvation from *sin*. There is salvation from *the wrath of God* during the Day of The Lord (1 Thessalonians 5:9). Israel will be saved *from their enemies* (Luke 1:71). There are three references to helmets of salvation in Scripture:

"For he put on righteousness as a breastplate and a helmet of salvation on his head" (Isaiah 59:17)

"But let us who are of the Day, be sober, putting on the breastplate of faith and love and as a helmet the hope of salvation" (1 Thessalonians 5:8).

This is linked to the Day of The Lord in verse 9.

"Take (*receive*, Greek *Dechomai*) the helmet of salvation" (Ephesians 6:17).

This by implication, refers to the *mind.*

6.

The Sword of
the Spirit

6. THE SWORD OF THE SPIRIT

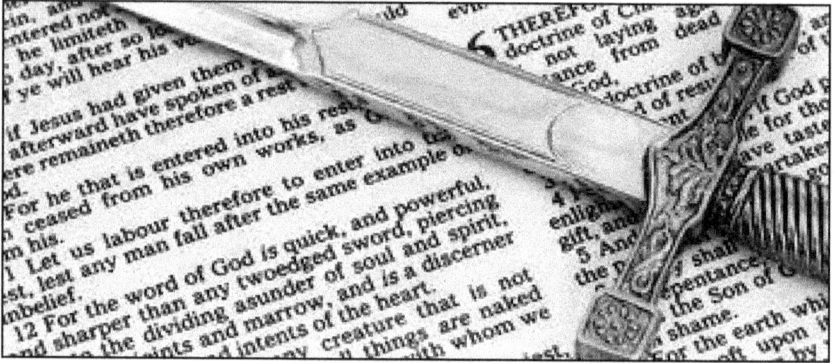

Now clothed in all parts of our spiritual armour, we may be entrusted with the sword, which is the Word of God. Sword play is an art, a skilled exercise. It is not for those who are unskilled in God's Word. It is a defensive weapon against the lies of the adversary, Satan. How sad it is to see the unskilful use of God's Word by some saints, who instead of using it against our adversary, Satan, *hack each other about!* The sword is to be used against wicked spirits, not our fellow human beings.

"For we do not wrestle against flesh and blood, but against principalities, against powers, against the rulers of the darkness of this age against the spiritual hosts of wickedness, in the heavenly realms." (Ephesians 6:12 RAV)

If you want to see a master Swordsman at work turn to Matthew 4:1-11. Notice the way our Lord parried the sword thrusts of Satan. *"It is written"* was the reply to all Satan's thrusts. The first test, (v 3), was to tempt our Lord to provide, by His own power, food for Himself, instead of depending upon God His Father above for sustenance. Our Lord's reply was

"*It is written* man shall not live by bread alone, but by every word that proceeds from the mouth of God." (v 4 RAV)

The next test was more subtle and occurred when our Lord and Satan were looking down from the height of a wing of the Sanctuary. Satan is adept at misquoting Scripture. He related a text which is perfectly true in its rightful place.

"If you are the Son of God, throw yourself down. For it is written, 'He shall give His angels charge concerning you and, in their hands they shall bear you up, lest you dash your foot against a stone'." (v 6 RAV)

Our Lord's reply was

"*It is written again* You shall not tempt The Lord your God". (v 7 RAV)

Christ would not go out of His way to find out if God would perform a miracle to save Him. This would imply doubt or unbelief on His part. The final test was from the top of a very high mountain, where Satan showed Christ all the kingdoms of the world and their glory,

"… and he (Satan) said to Him, all these things I will give you, if you will fall down and worship me." (vs 8-9 RAV)

This was no idle promise of Satan's. He is the god of this world and could have given our Lord all the kingdoms of this world and their glory. This Satan will do in the future to the man of sin, (Anti Christ, Satan's christ), *who will* bow down and worship him. The temptation was to avoid the sufferings of the cross and its shame, by accepting the kingdom at Satan's hands. Our Lord's reply was,

> "Away with you Satan! *For it is written* 'You shall worship the Lord your God and Him only you shall serve.'" (v 10 RAV)

Every quotation of Scripture by our Lord was pertinent to the sword thrusts of Satan, who was defeated on all counts and departed for a season.

The Armour of God   36

7.

Prayer

7. PRAYER

I have now briefly covered the six pieces of armour. There remains one more vital thing. The Ephesians saints were requested by Paul to pray for him and his ministry and for *all* saints. He asked for boldness to make known the secret of the gospel, which is the gospel of peace (v 16) the Conciliation of the world, incorporated into the secret administration relating to the Body of Christ, with its heavenly destiny. All those today, who seek to make known these precious truths, need our prayers, in this day of departure from the faith (2 Corinthians 5:8-21; Ephesians 1:3).

As I see it in Christendom today, much prayer is offered on behalf of the *physical* welfare of congregations, but prayers for wisdom to understand the unsearchable (untraceable CV) riches of Christ, do not seem to be uttered anywhere. Our calling, which is above in Christ Jesus, seems to be largely ignored. Let us consider Paul's closing benediction to this glorious epistle to the Ephesians,

> "Peace to the brethren, and love with faith, from God the Father and The Lord Jesus Christ." (v 33 RAV)

What a soothing word "peace" is! There is the peace that our Heavenly Father shows us and bids us show to our fellow men (Ephesians 6:15; 2 Corinthians 5:18-21). There is also:

> "the peace of God which surpasses all understanding (that is superior to every frame of mind CV), which will guard our

hearts and minds through Christ Jesus"
(Philippians 4:7 RAV).

"Peace perfect peace,
by thronging duties pressed,
To do the will of God, this is rest.
Peace perfect peace,
with sorrows swinging round,
In God's presence,
naught but calm is found."

"Grace be with all those who love our Lord
Jesus Christ in sincerity (incorruption).
Amen" (Ephesians 6:24 RAV)

All of God's Saints down through the ages, have
experienced a measure of His *grace,* but what of
us? Do we know something of the *superbounding*
grace of God and the love He lavishes on us, who
deserve it least of all! Let us revel in it and find its
satisfactory fulfilment in our own personal
experience.

Some of us may feel that we are "advanced" in our
knowledge of God's Word, that we understand

"Dispensational Truth" and can clearly see our heavenly calling in Christ Jesus, in the heavenly realms, (Philippians 3:20; Ephesians 1:3). This may cause the ugly head of pride to rear itself up.

Let us remember that the love of Christ, which passes all knowledge, is not diminished by one iota towards those who have not yet grasped by faith their calling which is in Christ Jesus.

Let us never look down on "babes in Christ", through the eyes of a proud Pharisee and with haughty superiority. Rather let us remember the time when we were also just "babes in Christ", until God opened our eyes, the eyes of our heart, and gave us spiritual understanding and wisdom in the deeper things of God. What we rejoice in was not received by our intellect, but given to us freely by God's Holy Spirit, Who alone gave us faith to believe Him.

Let us love *all* "who call on The Lord out of a pure (cleansed CV) heart" (2 Timothy 2:22). Some of them may avoid us and refuse our fellowship, but if they truly love our Lord in the light of the truth

God has revealed to them, may God's grace super-abound to them!

Conclusion

CONCLUSION

To conclude, I would like to summarise certain facts, relating to our heavenly warfare:-

- Our blessings are *spiritual* in Christ, in heavenly realms Our spiritual warfare is not against flesh and blood, but against the spiritual forces of wickedness in the heavenly realms.

- The attack of these spiritual forces cannot affect our Salvation or membership of the Body of Christ. All that is outside all possible attack as *we are in Christ.*

- The attack is against our *enjoyment by faith* of our heavenly possessions in *Christ Jesus:* the possibility of receiving a reward for faithful service (2 Timothy 4:7-8).

- The battleground is the body of death, the flesh which exists in all of us, which we inherit from Adam. Our foes, the wicked spirits in heavenly places, are under the command of Satan, the god of this age, who seek to attack us through the flesh.

- These foes do not exist at the right hand of God, where we are spiritually seated in Christ Jesus and will actually be there physically, when we are called on high (Colossians 3:1-4).

It is vitally important that we put on the whole armour of God, for without it we are defenceless against our spiritual foes in the heavenly realms.

MORE ON SALVATION

Salvation:

Safe and Secure

By Sylvia Penny

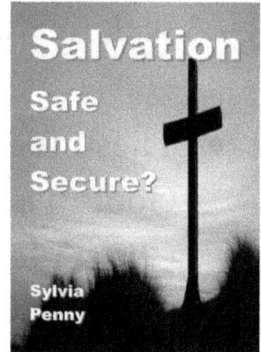

This important book is a thorough treatment of the subject of salvation, asking such questions as:

- What is it, exactly, that saves us?
- Is salvation secure?
- Can it be lost?
- What is 'conditional security'?

It deals with a wide number of issues such as:

- Salvation and works
- The doctrine of rewards
- Lordship salvation
- Free grace theology
- Assurance of salvation
- Why people lose their faith

Further details of all this book, and the ones on the following pages, can be seen on
www.obt.org.uk

They can be ordered from the website
and also from

The Open Bible Trust,
Fordland Mount, Upper Basildon,
Reading, RG8 8LU, UK.

They are also available as eBooks
from Amazon and Apple,
and also as KDP paperbacks from Amazon.

MORE ON EPHESIANS

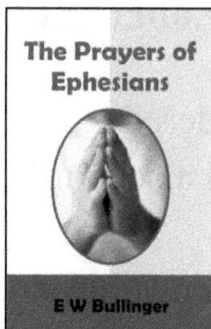

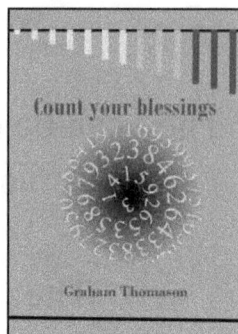

Spiritual Blessing in heavenly realms
Brian Sherring

Using Ephesians 1:3 as his starting point the author brings before the reader the spiritual blessing Paul goes on to write about.

The Prayers of Ephesians
E W Bullinger

This deals with the major prayers of chapters 1 & 3, and Paul's comments on prayer at the end of chapter 6.

Count your blessing
Graham Thomason

This majors on the blessing Christians have in Christ, many of which Paul wrote about in Ephesians

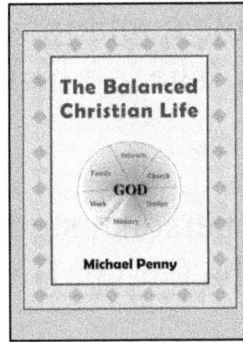

Sit, Walk, Stand

The Christian life in Ephesians

W M Henry and Michael Penny

- What have Christian in Christ that they can rest upon (Sit)?
- How should they live their lives (Walk)?
- What must they resist (Stand)?

The Balanced Christian Life

Michael Penny

A series of five studies based on Ephesians exploring …

The Blessings Christians have in Christ and The Practical Christian Life which should follow

This is a large book designed for individual or group work. The right hand pages ask questions, fill in Bible quotations and other open ended activities. The left hand pages contain the answers.

Ideal for personal study and for any Lent Group, Post Alpha Group, House Group or Bible Study Group.

If any organisations wish to use the diagrams and worksheets contained in this book they are free to copy them, and there is no need to seek permission.

That you may be filled

Charles Ozanne

The aim of this book is to investigate the unsearchable riches of Christ as found in Paul's most exalted epistle, Ephesians. By selecting some of the more significant passages Charles Ozanne has brought to light the unique message of this epistle.

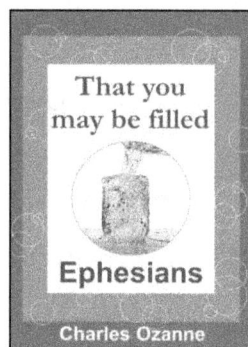

The author's hope is that having read this publication the reader will have a deeper understanding and a higher appreciation of God's purpose for this age of grace

FREE SAMPLE

For a free sample of
the Open Bible Trust's magazine *Search*,
please email

admin@obt.org.uk

or visit

www.obt.org.uk/search

ABOUT THE AUTHOR

James Poole was born in Finchley, London, in 1909 and took a course in Business Training at the City of London College. During his working years he was employed by various institutions and banks in the City of London. When he wrote this booklet he was enjoying retirement with his wife in Eastbourne, Sussex, but has since fallen asleep in Christ.

ALSO BY
JAMES POOLE

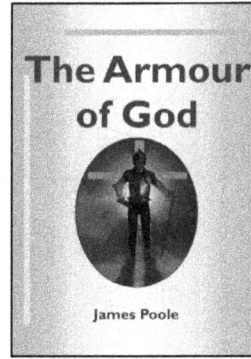

Abraham

James Poole

Isaac

James Poole

Jacob

James Poole

Joseph

James Poole

Notes on Ephesians

James Poole

The Armour of God

James Poole

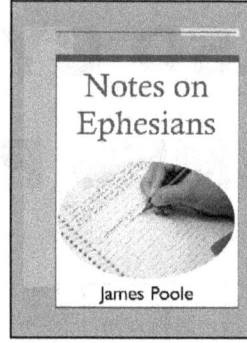

Further details of all the books here can be seen on **www.obt.org.uk**

The can be ordered from the website and also from

The Open Bible Trust,
Fordland Mount, Upper Basildon,
Reading, RG8 8LU, UK.

They are also available as eBooks
from Amazon and Apple,
and also as KDP paperbacks from Amazon.

FURTHER READING

Approaching the Bible
Michael Penny

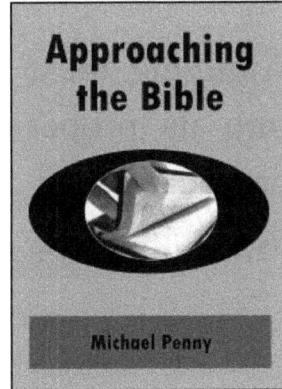

In easy to understand steps, and with many interesting examples, Michael Penny provides the rational for the view that before we try to *apply* any passage in the Bible to ourselves, we should discover first what it meant to those to whom its words were initially addressed. The book advocates that this is best done by considering the passage under the following headings:

1) **W**ho said or wrote it;
2) to **W**hom was it said or written, or concerning **W**hom was it said or written;
3) **W**here it was said or written, or concerning **W**here was it said or written;
4) **W**hat was said or written;

5) **When** was it said or written, or concerning **When** was it said or written;
6) **Why** was it said or written.

Applying these six **"W"** rules puts the passage into its proper context and gives us the right perspective on it. Only after doing this can we determine:

7) **Whether** the passage applies to our situation and what the correct application is.

It is the *consistent* use of these **Seven Ws** which helps us discover the right and relevant application of any passage to our lives.

****

This book, and the one on the next page, can be ordered from **www.obt.org.uk** and from

The Open Bible Trust,
Fordland Mount, Upper Basildon,
Reading, RG8 8LU, UK.

40 Problem Passages

Michael Penny

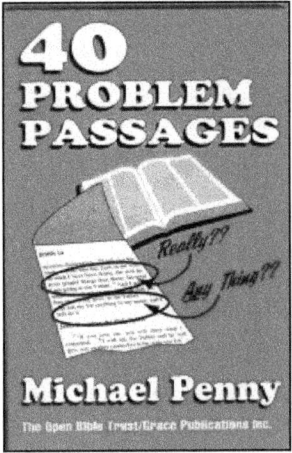

This book is a sequel to *Approaching the Bible*.

The 7 Ws advocated in *Approaching the Bible* are applied to 40 difficult to understand passages. There are, of course, far more than 40 Problem Passages in the Bible. However, in this book Michael Penny not only solves these *40 Problem Passages*, but in doing so he equips the reader with a method by which many, many more hard to understand and difficult passages can be understood and successfully applied to the life of the believer today.

✳✳✳✳✳✳✳✳✳✳✳✳✳✳✳✳✳✳✳✳

This book, and the ones on the previous pages,
are also available as eBooks
from Amazon and Apple,

and also as KDP paperbacks from Amazon.

The Armour of God   58

ABOUT THIS BOOK

THE ARMOUR
OF GOD

The closing section of Ephesians is one of the best known and most helpful passages in all Paul's writings. In it he wrote about:

- The belt of truth
- The breastplate of righteousness
- The sandals of peace
- The shield of faith
- The helmet of salvation
- The sword of the spirit

James Poole's clear and concise comments on these, and on Paul's closing words on *prayer,* are most helpful to every child of God who has, at times, found this life a battle.

Publications of The Open Bible Trust must be in accordance with its evangelical, fundamental and dispensational basis. However, beyond this minimum, writers are free to express whatever beliefs they may have as their own understanding, provided that the aim in so doing is to further the object of The Open Bible Trust. A copy of the doctrinal basis is available at

www.obt.org.uk/doctrinal-basis

or from:

THE OPEN BIBLE TRUST
Fordland Mount, Upper Basildon,
Reading, RG8 8LU, UK.

www.ingramcontent.com/pod-product-compliance
Lightning Source LLC
Chambersburg PA
CBHW060610030426
42337CB00018B/3020